DUBAI

Adam Jackson

A

Also by Bram Jackson

Zanzibar
The Ancestral Trip
Budget Bangkok
Budget New York

COPYRIGHT NOTICE

DUBAI

for those who dare to be
a stranger in somebody's home.

"Adventure is worthwhile"

- Aesop

Why Dubai?

The United Arab Emirates, in which Dubai is part of, is one of the most important countries in the Middle East. Interestingly enough, this is a new country with a history that dates back to thousands.

Mark Jonathan Beech, an archeologist with the University of York in the UK, found a 130,000-year-old rock knife in the area, arguing that human life has existed there at least as long.

Yet, the United Arab Emirates as a country was formed in 1971. Prior to that the country was under various rulers, most recently under the Ottoman Empire and later under the United Kingdom from which it got its independence.

Today the UAE is one of the most modern countries in the Middle East and has been an ally of the United States (and the West in general) for as long as anyone else.

Of the seven Emirates that make up the UAE it is without doubt that Dubai stands out. Although the entire UAE is oil-dependent in general, more and more Dubai is breaking away from that dependency. For several years now the Emirate has been recognized as a trade hub in the world, with its retail power falling behind only London.

"Dubai's global air connectivity and its growing stature as a hub for trade between the East and West has clearly given an added impetus to the retail sector," Nick Maclean told the *Arabian Business News* last year.

Maclean, who is the managing director of the Middle

Eastern division of the CBRE Group, which is an American commercial real estate company headquartered in Los Angeles, was discussing why Dubai holds the position for several years.

Dubai, which doesn't have as much as oil as Abu Dhabi, has been thinking outside the box for decades. It opened its doors to the international community. Today nearly 85% of the Emirate are people from international backgrounds.

As you walk through the city you are more prone to see foreigners rather than the locals. This is especially the case when you are anywhere in which you encounter workers, as the majority of the workers in the Emirate are from foreign backgrounds.

Dubai has worked hard to provide for its rich tourists with all the top-level experiences they could ever ask for. In the process millions of people from Asia and Africa provide the workface necessary to deal with it.

But don't think they are all cleaning toilets. Dubai's top job sectors for foreigners, according to *The Dubai Bizz*, are construction and real estate, hospitality and tourism, technology, and the financial sector.

"I will probably never be a citizen," said a young man from India, smiling, "I knew that when I came here. Dubai has given me a lot of options. My life is much better now than I think it could ever be back home in India."

This young man came to Dubai just eleven years ago. Today he has his own company in the Real Estate industry and partners with big money to manage luxury properties. He started out as the assistant to an agent he knew from back home, and through years skyrocketed through his career to become his own man.

Dubai is friendly to foreigners because the possibilities are endless. Many people who come to work for Dubai based companies generally find themselves being treated to a good life from the get go. That is what happened to a fresh-out-of-college British young man. He got a degree in tourism management and was recruited while in school.

"Flat and car were part of the package that attracted me," he said, laughing, "No one would ever offer me something like that in London! I would have been struggling to pay rent."

But it wasn't just about the luxury lifestyle alone for this young man. It was also the weather. Dubai has a sunny climate all year long. Compared to the gray skies of London he knew Dubai was going to offer sunshine and palm trees even in the wintertime.

"I would say that is a big reason a lot of people move here," said a Swedish woman who was considering moving to Dubai and was going around to companies, looking for a job. "The weather is incredibly nicer than Stockholm. In the winter it can be a great place to live. Of course, the summer is hot, really hot, but you have all the amenities to hide from the heat," she added.

Knowing its climate can be extreme in the summer months, sometimes reaching as hot as 115° F, the Emirate has done amazing job in creating tons of unique ways to escape the heat. There are literally indoor worlds that keep people entertained all day long.

So, you might be asking why Dubai? Why not! It is a beautiful location with a beautiful forward thinking. It has opportunities for everyone. It is welcoming.

Through this book, I hope, you learn what you need to check out Dubai!

Dubai is Safe

Suicide bombings ripped through Istanbul in 2003 between November 13 and November 20th, leaving 57 people dead and around 700 others injured. Less than six months before there was a suicide bombing in Saudi Arabia that left 91 people dead, according to the *Daily Mail*. The year before 238 people were killed in suicide bombings in Israel.

In the meantime resorts in countries like Egypt and Tunisia have been hit by terrorism, leaving countless people dead and injured in the process.

Dubai, on the other hand, has been safe.

The U.S. Department of State's Bureau of Consular Affairs, while warning Americans of the danger in traveling in the Middle East, admits that the local "law enforcement units have effectively demonstrated the capacity to detect, deter, and prevent acts of terrorism."

That includes a terrorist threat thwarted in 2012.

"Al-Qaeda and other terrorist groups have largely left the emirate alone even while hitting other major cities and resorts in the Middle East," notes Michael Baker in an article for *The Arizona Republic.*

Dubai's safety is part of its overall objective to be a different place in the Middle East. The majority of its population is not even Middle Eastern. According to the Dubai Statistics Center approximately 70% of Dubai's population are mainly individuals whose ethnic backgrounds are in India and the Philippines.

Baker notes that both violent and property crimes are rare. The United Nations Office on Drugs and Crime (UNODC) says murder rate in Dubai is less than 3 per 100,000. This rate is only half of the global average, meaning Dubai is much safer than other cities of its size.

"No one dares do anything stupid here," says an American executive who has lived here for nearly 10 years. "I think the Sharia laws they have here are very severe when it comes to violent crimes, and I do believe that deters people from committing them."

Although Dubai is a cosmopolitan Emirate full of global people it is still a Middle Eastern place that deals with local religions and traditions. Islam is the main religion here and the country has laws that blend both Western and Islamic traditions.

In other words Dubai offers a safe city from both local and global criminals.

However, just because you are safe from the local and the international criminals doesn't mean you're safe from the local laws. What makes Dubai safe, according to that American, is also what makes Dubai the kind of place one has to make sure to pay attention to the rules.

A few years ago a Norwegian woman named Marte Deborah Dalelv had come to Dubai for business. She had arrived from neighboring Qatar where she had been based. She reported to the police that she was raped by a colleague and ended up getting arrested and facing jail time for unlawful sex, illegal consumption of alcohol, and for making false statements to the police. Dalelv, who is an interior designer, was later pardoned by Dubai's ruler.

The episode shocked the international community and reminded people that Dubai, despite its Vegas-like experiences, is very much a product of its environment.

"You have to be careful where you go, what you do, and to whom you speak and in which manner," says the American executive. "I learned over the years that Dubai is a wonderful place if you are a good guest and mind your steps. It is actually easy to do once you get used to it."

In other words one should be respectful of the local culture and law. There are too many foreigners who visit or live here, and it only goes to show you that it is a safe place.

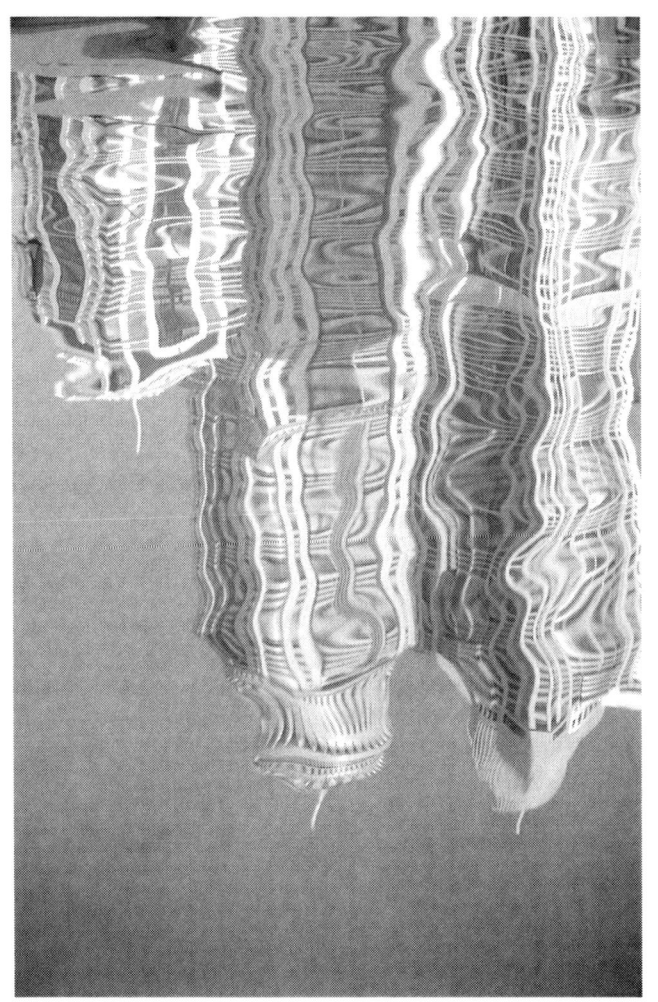

"Traveling turns you into a storyteller"

- Ibn Battuta

Be Careful

Although Dubai is safe one should still be careful. You are in a foreign society. Here are some tips to keep you safe:

Keep Yourself in the Loop - Make sure to listen to the radio and watch television news, as locally as you can, if you have access. You can also keep in touch with the Emirate through the Internet. Being in the loop allows you to be aware of possible dangers in the works.

People in Dubai generally know when something is coming, and therefore just pay attention and watch them. Also, make sure you're accessible to your hotel at any moment since they will contact you if there are any dangers out there.

For example, you may not know who Salman Khan is. Bollywood superstar Salman Khan is a famous figure to the

Emirate's Indian population. In 2011 he caused stampede at the premiere of his film 'Ready' in Dubai at the Grand Cineplex.

Don't Wander on Your Own - Even though they Emirate's natural beauty might invite you to get lost in the desert. Please, don't. If you come to Dubai on your own, make sure to stay at a hotel that can arrange your needs and align you with groups.

When in Doubt, Take a Taxi - This is really important anywhere in the world. If your gut is telling you don't walk, don't walk. That said, any time late night it is best to take a taxi rather than tempt fate. Neighborhoods that are perfectly safe in the day (when most teens are in school or because of fear of broad daylight) can turn unsafe in the dark. If you're going to an event at night, sometimes your hotel can arrange for you to go with a group, especially if the event is something interesting to most tourists.

Make Sure the Taxi is Real - Private cars, rented cars, commercial transport vehicles and private company vehicles are found to be involved in carrying passengers illegally. Dubai's Road and Transport Authority (RTA) says the practice is dangerous for the passengers and hurts the local economy and reputation. The drivers are fined 5000 AED (about $1,500). Despite this there are drivers who do this, some of them who had taken large sums of money in advance from unsuspecting people and disappeared.

Dress (and act) Modestly - As a Muslim society Dubai expects its guests to be modest. In their terms, as shown in some signs. When you enter certain establishments there are signs that tell the customers to cover the shoulders and knees.

If you visit any places of worship, make sure to be silent, switch off your cellphone, and do not eat or drink, and certainly no smoking.

Of course, when you're in the safe areas of your guided tour or in your hotel things are different. So, check in with your hotel to make sure what applies to you. When you are out and about, don't expose too much skin.

Respect the Simplicity - You will note that many men and women in Dubai are traditionally dressed, generally in black clothes for women and white for men. Even though they may be wearing clothes that look simple remember it can be very expensive designer brands.

And here are some health tips:

Stick to Bottled Water – Although the drinking water in Dubai is pretty clean, and the Emirate works hard to keep it that way, it doesn't mean your stomach will agree with it. There are toxins in the ground because of pollution and water from the tap might have some of it that your stomach will say, "Oh, no!"

As such, do what most people in Dubai do and drink your water from a bottle.

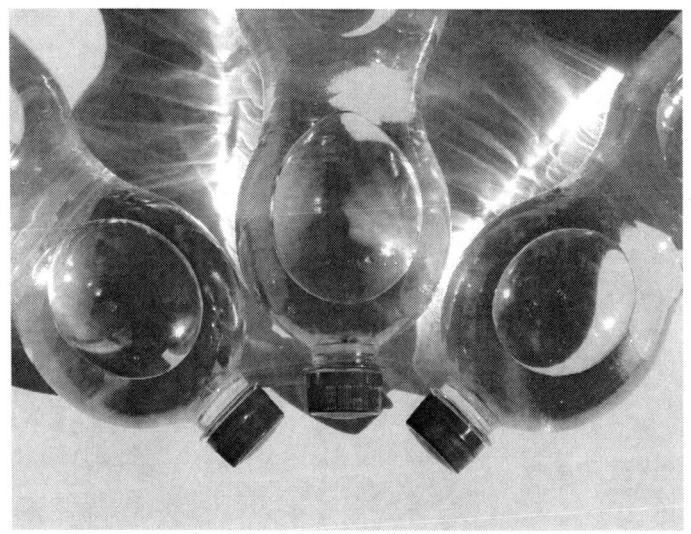

Of course, drinking bottled water in the high heat of the desert poses its own risks. If the plastic bottle is made from Bisphenol A or BPA, which has been known to release harmful chemicals into any substance it contains, you might want to make sure it is not left in the sun too long.

Be Conscious of Malaria - Malaria, which is caused by some types of the plasmodium parasite and is spread by the bites of infected mosquitos, is a big problem in Africa and Asia, continents that supply a lot of people with Dubai.

In 2007 the World Health Organization declared Dubai to be Malaria-free zone. However, that seemed to have been a case of jumping the gun. In a December 2011 article *Gulf News* reported on the rise of new malaria cases, and especially cases recognized to have been local rather than the usual imported cases from Africa and Asia.

"The stagnant waters are mosquito-breeding grounds. People get bitten and fall sick. When I test them, it turns out to be malaria," Dr. Fouziya Ayyub told the paper.

In the meantime, bring mosquito repellents, especially those with DEET or N-Diethyl-meta-toluamide. Although this chemical is toxic, which normally you would not want to use without a real need, it is the only thing that really works on mosquitoes.

"We travel, some of us forever, to seek other places, other lives, other souls."

– Anais Nin

Dubai Basics

Dubai, as part of the United Arab Emirates, uses the following UAE items:

The currency is called **United Arab Emirates Dirham**, and many people will refer to it simply as Dirham, with International code of **AED**. As of February 15, 2016 the $1 equals to about 3.67 AED. The Dirham ranges from 25 fils, a coin, to 1,000 Dirham notes.

Photo © Toumi Fethi.

If you need to make calls to the locals you would need to dial **+971**, the International Code for UAE. That is in the United States you would dial 011 + 971 + local number.

Emergency phone number in UAE is **999**, the equivalent of 911.

The local time is **GMT+4**, which means it is about 9 hours ahead of Eastern Standard Time. That is, 10PM EST would be 7AM local time in Dubai.

"To be interested in the changing seasons is a happier state of mind than to be hopelessly in love with spring"

– George Santayana

When to Go

Like any place on this beautiful planet Dubai has good, bad, and ugly periods. The good news about Dubai, located in the hot Middle East, is that it really is warm all year long.

You will never have to worry about your feet being so cold like during the winters in the northern hemisphere. Furthermore, the greenery of the Arabian Peninsula is always there. It is such a beautiful sight.

That, however, does not mean it is pleasant all year long. To give you a summary of what I will tell you below, which I hope you take the time to go through, basically avoid Dubai three periods of the year, if you can:

1) The first period to avoid is during the sandstorm season, known as *shamal*, which happen both in winter and

summer—causing serious issues for the locals and tourists;

2) Second period to avoid is during Ramadan, which is the fasting month for Muslims and when religious piety is an all-time high.

3) And the third period is the summer season when temperatures can hit three digits and humidity is very high, as this season limits outdoor activities

Go in the Winter

The best time to visit Dubai is the winter season. Although months between November and March are generally the recommended times, in reality one should try to go there from November to January (because of the *shamal* or sandstorm season).

This is a nice time of the year because the weather is cool, the sun is not torching, and there is very little rain. This is a period that is not very humid. Normally the temperatures for this period range from 75 to 85 Degrees Fahrenheit or 24 to 30 Degrees Celsius.

The winter is what I would call the high season. It is the time of the year when the majority of the tourist attractions are in full swing. Many tourists prefer to come during this period simply because of the weather.

The winter is a harsh time in Europe, as it is in North

America, and there are cheap flights if one can book in advance. For example, a *SunExpress* flight from London to Dubai in March 2017 was just $140 if booked a year in advance.

As such Dubai sees a lot of European tourists during the winter months. The United Kingdom, with only Saudi Arabia and India ahead, was the leader of the non-regional countries that supplied visitors to Dubai in 2014.

The United States, Germany, and China are also all in the top ten.

That means if you go during that time make sure to book your trip way in advance, to avoid the high prices that visitors from developed countries are welcomed with.

Shamal

The *shamal*, which is characterized by strong winds that whip the Arabian Desert into blinding sandstorms, is probably the worst thing that can ever happen to you in Dubai as a tourist. The sandstorm is caused by northern ("shamal" means "north" in Arabic) winds that blow from as far as Syria and Jordan.

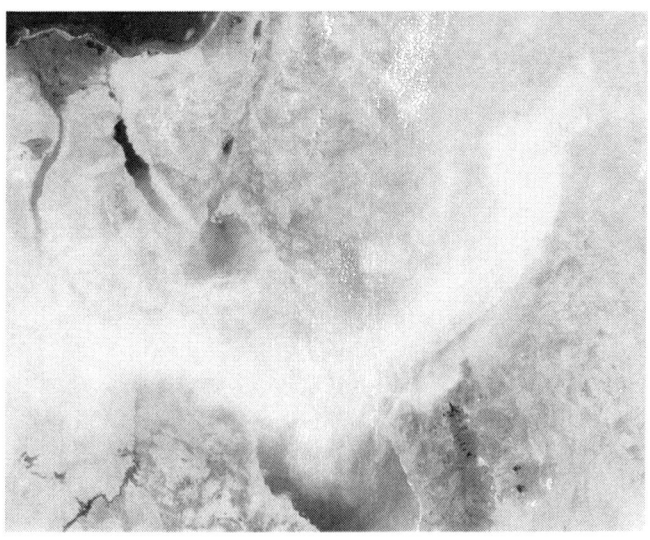

These winds can last for several days and can cause a lot of problems for both locals and tourists. People who have asthma, for example, are affected because of the loose particles in the storm. Shamal sandstorms have also caused deaths in accidents caused by the low visibility.

Of course, Dubai is in the desert and sandstorms can happen anytime. However, it has been reported that it generally happens during the winter and summer. January 28,

2011, February 26, 2012, and April 2, 2015 were all recent dates when strong sandstorms caused issues in Dubai.

Now, it should be noted that the Arabian Desert is generally nice. It's quiet and people use it for all sorts of recreational activities, aside from the people who actually live there. So, this is not to discourage you form having a good time. Just be careful.

Ramadan

The *Ramadan* is a holy season for Muslims that lasts for an entire period of thirty days. It occupies the ninth month of the Muslim calendar. On the Gregorian calendar it falls on different periods.

In 2016 it was first week June to first week July. In 2017 it falls on May 27th to June 25th, more or less as it can be a day before or day after. The best thing to do, if you are not a Muslim, is to call the local Islamic center or mosque and ask them when Ramadan is for that year.

During Ramadan most Muslims will abstain from food and water from sunrise to sunset. For Muslims Ramadan is not fasting for fun, it is a period of prayer, fasting, charity giving and self-accountability. As a predominantly Muslim country many businesses in the United Arab Emirates are shortened or closed during the day, including restaurants or cafes.

People tend to be more religious during Ramadan period and are far less forgiving of cultural mistakes a tourist might make. As such, unless you are a Muslim, I don't think it is a good period to visit Dubai for tourism.

That said, if you need to go there for business or want to go back and experience Ramadan in Dubai I would recommend the following:

Be Respectful - People are fasting. Even if they are doing it for spiritual purposes they are still human and are, therefore, hungry. Try to avoid eating or drinking in public during the daylight hours.

If you're staying at a hotel chances are the restaurant at your hotel will be open. That, of course, also means some of the people working there will be fasting. In Dubai many people are from non-Muslim countries. However, most locals fast even if they are not religious most of the year. It is much more than a religious act, it is cultural also.

As such, I talked to people who are not Muslim put who respect this practice and actually fast. Therefore, I recommend that you order your meal through room service.

Be Locally Modest - I don't like to tell people this. Modesty is a subjective ideology. What is modest in California is obviously different from Dubai. So, as the old saying goes, when in Rome do as the Romans.

Dubaians are modern people in the 21st Century, like most people, but most of them do belong to traditional Muslim branches. As such you should cover as much as you can, but for sure follow Visit Dubai's suggestion to cover the shoulders and knees and to wear loose-fitting clothes.

Do Iftar - Muslims break their fast after sunset, or what the locals call *iftar*. Many locals have elaborate feast to break their fast, and if you happen to know someone who belongs to such a family it can be a great experience.

Shop – Midway into Ramadan, you will already note the busy shopping period that slowly gets more and more chaotic as time goes on. That is because those two weeks are like the two weeks before Christmas. Everyone needs to get their shopping done, and the good prices are rolled in.

Stay for Eid - Eid celebrates the end of a successful fasting period. Eid is worthy of extending your stay. Dubai is full of color and happiness is everywhere. Lots of special foods are made, some of which are Eid-only stuff, including sweets. Eid celebrations in Dubai last for days. As such, if you're there towards the end of the Ramadan season I would strongly urge you to stay for it.

"Travel is the only thing you buy that makes you richer."

– Anonymous

Before You Go

Before you go off to your trip there are a few things I would like you to keep in mind, as they will make your trip smoother in the long run.

GSM Phone – Do you have a GSM-based phone? If not, you can buy one via Amazon.com for less than $15. Since 2014 most phones (90%) are GSM-based.

However, if you happen to be one of the people still on that 10% it would be best to get a GSM phone. Most Apple and Android based phones are GSM phones.

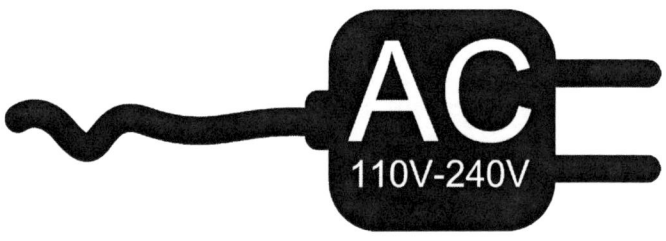

Electronic Extras – Make sure to bring your own chargers, adapters, and converters. There are many shops here in Dubai to get anything, including at the airport, but in case you arrive late night or something, make sure to bring what you need.

Keep in mind that in the United Arab Emirates the

voltage is 220-240, 50 Cycles. For American products that are 110V you would need an adapter. The socket type is the three pin British system. The prongs are square.

Medications – Although Dubai, like many areas of the Middle East, has good pharmacies I would suggest to bring your own medications.

Make sure to visit your doctor and let him or her know you're traveling. Fill any prescription medications you get for travel diseases before you leave.

Bring Goodies – If you can try to bring things you will need for your trip but that you can leave behind for the nice people you will meet. This includes any old phones you might have, clothes that you don't wear often, or anything else that you could use for your trip but can donate at the end. It will mean so much to the poor people who will clean your hotel bed!

"He who would travel happily must travel light."

– Antoine de St. Exupery

How to Get There

Dubai is not as far as you think. A flight from London reaches Dubai about an hour less than it would take to get to New York. In other words, it would take about seven hours. If you're smart, you may not even end up dealing with nasty travel side effects like jetlag.

There are nonstop flights from most of major European markets to Dubai. As such, travel between Europe and Dubai is painless.

If you are traveling from the United States, it is not that bad either. Emirates, the UAE based airline, has flights from all over the states, which means there are also nonstop flights to Dubai from most major markets. However, unfortunately, a flight from New York City to Dubai is about twelve and half hours to thirteen hours!

Depending on what time of day you fly, John F. Kennedy airport is the only one in the New York area that has nonstop flights to Dubai.

If you were flying from Chicago, it would be around fourteen hours. Emirates is the only airline that flies nonstop, and its flights travel from O'Hare airport.

Los Angeles to Dubai, which believe it or not many people take, is about sixteen hours when you fly nonstop.

Now that you know how easy it is to go, let's see if you can actually go.

Visa

Most people in the world need visa to enter the country unless you are traveling as an official, diplomat, or a member of financial groups like the World Bank or IMF.

Visa requirements for the United Arab Emirates is very minimal, provided you qualify.

Visa is not required for citizens of Saudi Arabia, Kuwait, Qatar, Bahrain, and Oman. These countries have special relationship with the country – they are all part of the Gulf Cooperation Council – and therefore benefit from a host of privileges.

Western nations also, as you would expect, tend to have a good deal not just in the United Arab Emirates but most of the Gulf countries.

The United States, Canada, countries in the European Union, Australia, Japan, and many other countries have good diplomatic relationship with the UAE and therefore visa is not required in advance for these citizens.

Those of you American and European Union members should know that visa is available to some citizens when they arrive at any port of entry. That said, however, visas on arrival are only good for those of you visiting for less than a month.

If you plan to visit longer than that, you have two options: 1) ask the immigration officer at the airport to extend your visa; 2) go to the central police station and ask to have your visa extended.

Regardless of your stay you will need two things when

you enter UAE: 1) you need to make sure your passport is valid for at least six months; 2) you must have a travel out of the UAE planned, whether a round-trip ticket or leaving to another destination.

If you're planning to go there for work, call the UAE's embassy in your capital or the nearest consulate.

To Dubai

The Dubai International Airport, whose international airport code is DXB, which is what you probably see on your ticket from your destination, is the busiest airport in the world. In 2015 there were nearly 80 million passengers who traveled through it.

It is also the busiest airport for cargo in the region, with only Chinese and American airports beating it to the top spot, as it handles most of the cargo for Africa and Middle East.

The airport is pretty modern in its features. It is probably your first entrance into the lavish world that is Dubai. There are currently three terminals:

Terminal 1 is home to international flights except Emirates Airlines. American airlines like Delta and United have their flights in and out of Terminal 1.

Terminal 2 is generally business and local, as well as low-budget airlines.

If you flew in with Emirates Airlines then you would becoming through Terminal 3, which is where the airline is based.

The airport is only 3 miles (or 5 km) away from the city center has several options to get you to your hotel. You can rent a car through any of the well-known car rental agencies such as Avis, Hertz, or even Thrifty.

Another popular option is to take a taxi. The cream colored taxis have two color trims: the red is the one driven by men, and accounts for most taxis; and females drive the ones with pink trim.

Taxis cost AED 25 (about $7) surcharge from the airport, which is added on top of your bill at the end of your trip, and AED 2 per each kilometer after. The good thing about the taxis is that they are available 24/7.

Even more options include subway. The red line goes through both Terminal 1 and Terminal 3. You can take that and if you need it will intersect with the green line at Union Square and Khalid Bin Al Waleed stations.

The Metro fare is AED 14 (around $3) for an all-day ticket. The metro starts at 5am and stops at Midnight.

Another option is to take a bus. The bus is the cheapest way to get around in Dubai. A trip from the airport to downtown hotel will cost you only AED 5 (or about $1.50). The buses leave in front of Terminals 1, 2, and 3.

Finally, a new service by the government of Dubai is what they are calling the Sky Bus Service, which is a bus service that has interesting things like snacks. If you flew with an airline that did not feed you, now will be your chance to eat something.

However, the Sky Bus Service is actually a good way to travel, as it will take you directly to the main hotels. There are 12 routes and costs about AED 15 (or about $3).

Start taking pictures because Dubai only gets better from the airport forward.

"One's destination is never a place, but a new way of seeing things."

– Henry Miller

Where to Stay

Dubai attracts millions of tourists from all over the world. Some of these tourists are super rich and can afford five star hotels & resorts. Others are on medium budget and can afford good hotels. Of course, there are also those who are on a low budget and can afford a decent place to stay.

What to keep in mind is that the economies are all relative. You might be able to pay a $100 and get a motel in San Francisco, but a $100 will go a long way in Dubai.

On the other hand, if you are a poor tourist who normally would stay at a cheap hostel in San Francisco you might be able to afford a decent hotel in Dubai.

Photo © Sarah Ackerman.

As such, where to stay really all depends on what you can afford.

There is something I want the reader to know, though.

When you stay at any of these "inclusive" places in Dubai, and thee are many of those at every budget, whatever money you spend will hardly make it to the poor people.

How can you offset this economical disadvantage? By hiring the poor whenever you can for all of your "extra" activities. By visiting local places.

By having "extra" meals at local restaurants. If there is anything that is charged extra you can rest be assured that there will be a local to provide it.

Photo © Braxmeier & Steinberger GbR.

Luxury

Dubai is a beautiful location full of beautiful hotels and resorts. The **Jumeirah Beach Hotel** is truly a beautiful hotel. It is located in Dubai's Umm Suqeim, a neighborhood in the western part of the city.

Photo © Alberto Gonzalez Rovira.

The hotel, which has its own waterpark known as the Wild Wadi, costs from about $2,000 to $15,000 per week during the high season. This five-star hotel has the beach as its backyard.

The **Taj Dubai** is a luxury hotel right in downtown Dubai. It has direct views of Burj Khalifa. This modern hotel offers many luxurious amenities in its five-star service. The Presidential Suite will set you back over $35,000 for a week during the high season.

In the artificial archipelago Palm Jumeirah you will find the **Atlantis The Palm**, a gorgeous resort that combines mythical and modern architecture. It offers stunning views of the Arabian Gulf. It has everything you need to enjoy a few days of sun and sea. The Royal Bridge Suite, which has 360-degree ocean-views, will cost over $100,000 for a week during the high season at this five-star hotel.

There are luxury hotels all over Dubai. Some of them you can book on your own, others are so exclusive you need to get in touch with them directly.

Photo © Henrik Bach Nielsen.

Medium

Located in the tax-free zone Dubai Media City, an area part of the Dubai Marina district, **Media One Hotel** is a good a medium budget in a popular area. 260 rooms, a very nice gym, an amazing pool with palm trees, what more can you ask from a $100-$250 nightly priced hotel? What about free access to Zero Gravity, the popular exclusive beach club, bar and restaurant, located only 5-7 minutes away from hotel!

Beach Hotel Apartments is in the cool Jumeira neighborhood, just a few minutes from the Jumeira Public Beach. Its 36 rooms come with full kitchens in a Turkish inspired architecture. There is a rooftop pool, with palm trees, giving you panoramic views of the Arabian Gulf. A seven-day stay during the high season will cost around $1,000.

Located in the historic area of Deira, the **Carlton Tower Hotel** overlooks the Dubai Creek and is just a few minutes walk from the beach. This is a very good option, especially because it is the lower end of the medium price range. It has a rooftop pool with sun-lounger terrace, and some of its 150-plus rooms have panoramic views of the city. A seven-day stay at this modest hotel during the high season will only cost you $700.

There are many medium budget hotels all over Dubai. In fact, the majority of the hotels in the city fall in this range, with over 500 hotels costing less than $200 a night. You can get more of them through hotel booking websites. However, one should keep in mind that in Dubai many hotels charge extras that you won't know until you've booked unless you're paying attention. For example, many hotels charge a 10% Municipality fee, AED 15.00 Tourism fee per night, as well as a 10% service charge.

Photo © Landmark Hotels & Suites.

Cheap

When it comes to Dubai, nothing is really "cheap." And even if it's normally expensive you can still experience "WOW!" factor for less, provided you're a smart shopper. Take the **Landmark Grand Hotel** in Deira, for example. This modern 4-star hotel offers spacious rooms, 24-hour room service and an outdoor swimming pool. It is perfectly located steps from the Union Metro Station and Al Ghurair Mall. A stay 7-day stay in a standard double room in the high season will only cost you a little less than $650 if booked in advance.

Other luxury hotels that recently were advertised for less than $700 included the **Hyatt Place Dubai Baniyas Square**, **Ramada Chelsea Hotel Al Barsha**, and **The Country Club Hotel Dubai**.

Just book in advance.

In the meantime, if you're short on time and you didn't

have a chance to book something luxurious in advance for less, you still have a lot of other options.

The **Dubai Nova Hotel**, in Bur Dubai neighborhood, is a two-star hotel that gives you a lot for your buck. The hotel has 84 rooms, with standard rooms coming with classic décor, air-condition, minibar, and satellite TV. A 7-day stay in the high season was recently advertised for $550.

Sahil Hotel in Deira goes for around $400 in the high season for a 7-day stay in a double room. This modest hotel has 35 rooms, all of which are air-conditioned, and is very conveniently located just couple of minutes from the Gold Souk. It has a 24-hour front desk, in case you get in late or you're the partying type. Although there isn't a restaurant in the hotel, the staff will get you something from nearby restaurants if you like.

Photo © Eric Gross.

How to Connect

Now that you arrived safely, and found your hotel, let's look at how you can stay connected. Almost all the hotels in Dubai have Wi-Fi. So, if you happen to have a smartphone or tablet or laptop, then you are covered in that sense.

If you happen to be a real adventurer and you left your equipment behind then you can use their computers to get on your social media to let your friends and family know you have made it.

Otherwise, you are also connected at most of the "nice" restaurants, cafes, as well as malls and even bars, as they will also offer you Wi-Fi.

If you want to be the King or Queen of your own connectivity, then don't you worry; Dubai is full of small and large companies that will help you do just that.

OneSimCard - If you do have or get a GSM phone, then you might want to check out US-based Belmont Telecom's *OneSimCard* service, which is an international cellular service you get so that you have the same phone number wherever you go (it works in most countries).

They assign you an Estonian-based number (area code +372), which is a European Union number so that people at home can call you cheaper. For example, someone from the United States could call you over Skype for just $0.02.

Yet, their "United Arab Emirates SIM Card" is exclusive service for this region and is specifically made for people who will be making international calls, aside from their local connections. With this service there is not any contracts, you pay only for the calls you make, and you get free incoming calls in the UAE from 165 countries, as well as free in coming SMS text messages in UAE and worldwide. If you do make a call, it will cost about $0.55 per minute. If you do text, it will cost you around $0.15.

If you happen to travel with another *OneSimCard* holder, calling them would cost about $0.25. Similarly, you would get all incoming SMS/texts for free. If you do send a text, it would still cost you about $0.15.

OneSimCard is not best when it comes to Internet. Their web charges are $15.50 per megabyte/MB. If you watched 1-minute video on YouTube it would be 2 to 5 megabytes/MB.

Du - If you still want a local company, then *Du* is the most recommended. Their "Tourist Plan" pre-paid service allows you to pay AED 55 (around $15) and get 20 minutes of calling time, 200MB mobile data and free vouchers from Uber, The Entertainer & Dollar Rent a Car worth AED 1,500 ($400). For extra service, *Du* costs AED 0.60 ($0.15) per minute, and AED 0.18 ($.05) for texting. For data, you would have to pay AED 55 to get the same amount or pay AED 1 ($0.25) per each megabyte.

Du, whose legal name actually is *Emirates Integrated Telecommunications Company*, is based in Dubai. The Al Salam Tecom Tower in Dubai Media City houses its offices. It is the second largest mobile provider in the country, and is co-owned by the UAE government, which owns about

40% of the company. The public shareholders own the rest, and the company is listed on the DFM or the Dubai Financial Market.

Etisalat - This is another local company. Their "Visitor line" service allows you to pay AED 100 (around $25) and get 44 minutes of calling time, 1GB mobile data and 5 hours over *Etisalat* Wi-Fi during a 14-day period. For extra service, *Etisalat* costs AED 0.60 ($0.15) per minute, and AED 0.18 ($.05) for texting. For data, you would have to pay AED 75 to get the same amount or pay AED 1 per each megabyte.

Etisalat, whose legal actually is *Emirates Telecommunications Corporation*, is the largest mobile provider in the country. It is a multinational company, but is also co-owned by the UAE government, which owns about 40% of the company. The public shareholders own the rest, and the company is based in Abu Dhabi and is listed on the ADX or Abu Dhabi Securities Exchange.

Photo © Beth Carey.

"Travel makes one modest. You see what a tiny place you occupy in the world."

– Gustave Flaubert

What to See

Dubai is an incredible place to visit. It is a place where the old and the new intermingle. Because of this mixture, which happens so naturally and organically, Dubai has something for everyone. Are you an architectural freak? Dubai will wow you! Are you the kind of person who loves to shop? You will be exhausted by all of the unique things you will find here! Are you into nature? One of the world's oldest natural phenomenons, the Arabian Desert, is here!

There are many things to see in Dubai, and many other places in the Emirates. For many reasons, including general safety, I would recommend going with a tour group, whether small or large. The larger the group the cheaper it will be. You can hire tour guides just for you.

If you are staying at a decent hotel chances are they will have access to a tour guide or group. If you are staying in an all-inclusive hotel or resort it will probably be included in your cost.

Nevertheless, you can also do this on your own.

I believe in walking tours because I think you get to see the area differently. You are taking in all the sights slowly before, during, and after your actual visit.

Another great thing about walking tours, especially ones you do with the least amount of people, is that you get to meet people.

I think people feel more comfortable and come up to you a lot faster than if you're in an organized group.

DOWNTOWN DUBAI

In Dubai, the first thing you want to see, and which probably will be the first thing you see, is **Downtown Dubai**. It is home to three interesting places: Burj Khalifa, Dubai Mall, and Dubai Fountain.

That is, Downtown Dubai represents everything that is "new" in this Emirate.

Photo © Guilhem Vellut.

The best way to see the places of importance in this area is a walking tour, which normally will last for about three hours or so. In other words, with waiting and traveling and eating, it will be about half a day.

Photo © Christian van Elven.

Walking Tour

A walking tour will cost you anywhere from $5 to $50, depending on who you hire and when. For example, a young immigrant, or a foreign student, and who speaks perfect English will charge you just $5; while a more structured tour with a reputable company will charge you about $25 to $50 if you go with a group. In low season months, especially months in which there aren't any big events, tour companies can be a good bargain, too.

Photo © Neekoh Fi.

Like I said earlier I think walking tours give you a better chance of meeting locals than if you are part of a large group. Think about you, would you rather talk to someone who is with a lot of people or someone who is with his or her significant other? It doesn't matter where you start, but I recommend your Downtown Dubai walking tour like this:

Photo © Ronald Musni.

Burj Khalifa

The. Tallest. Building. In. The. World. That is why you start with Downtown Dubai because it is home to the magnificent **Burj Khalifa**, a mega structure that will leave you breathless. If Dubai is defined by anything, it is that this is a city that pushes the boundaries.

Photo © Gary Bembridge.

The Dubai-based Emaar Properties developed it, and its architect and structural engineer were from the Chicago-based Skidmore, Owings & Merrill.

Construction began in 2004, and the building opened to the public in 2010.

With 163 floors above the ground, 154 of them usable, it really is an awesome structure to look at.

The Dubai Mall

If there is a shopper's heaven then it truly is **The Dubai Mall**, which is the largest mall in the world. In 2011 it was the most visited building on earth, having had over 50 million people go through its doors.

Developed by the same company that developed the Burj Khalifa, there is so much stuff at this mall that actually anyone could have fun—and not just the shoppers!

Photo © Patrik Carlsson.

With over 1200 stores, ranging from super high-end global brand names to unknown chic boutiques, it offers every shopper a chance to find whatever it is that they desire to purchase.

Along the way, of course, the shoppers are met with all kinds of entertainment. Like a Vegas casino, the Dubai Mall will help you forget time and let you loose in the midst of equally excited peers.

Some of the entertainment offered by the mall includes the **Dubai Aquarium & Underwater Zoo**, which is now one of the most famous spaces of its kind. It is home to around 300 species. What are some of the interesting ones? How about a shark!

Yes, a shark at your mall.

Photo © Steve Douglas.

With 270-degree acrylic walk-through tunnel, this is definitely one of the more fun places you will ever stop by between your shopping and dining.

The 80,000 sq ft interactive mini-city **KidZania** is truly something any child will enjoy. As an "edutainment" you will feel relaxed that your kid is also being educated.

Other attractions include the **Rainforest Cafe, SEGA Republic,** and the **Dubai Ice Rink.**

Dubai Fountain

Truly, one of the magnificent things in Dubai is the **Dubai Fountain**, which is located on the 30-acre manmade Burj Khalifa Lake, and is believed to be the largest choreographed fountain system in the world.

Designed by the same firm that designed the fountain at the Bellagio Hotel in Las Vegas, the Dubai Foundatin can shoot straight up in the air up to 500 feet!

Photo © Steven Byles.

Why is this an important attraction? Well, there are choreographed performances that should be checked out. The majority of these performances take place in the evening, but since you're doing your walking tour in the day you should check out the two performances in the day at 1pm and at 1:30pm.

The first show of the day starts with "Sama Dubai," a

tribute to Dubai's ruler Sheikh Mohammed, a song performed by Emerati folk singer Mehad Hamad.

You can listen to the song in advance on YouTube, and get the lyrics from the Internet.

In the evening, starting at 6pm, there are shows every 30 minutes until 10pm during the week (Satuday through Thursday), and until 11pm on the weekends (Thursday and Friday).

Souk Al Bahar

Dubai Fountain leads you to the Fountain Bridge, which leads you to **Souk Al Bahar**. This market, which in Arabic means "market of the sailor," seeks to give the tourist a glimpse of what an Arab markets is like.

Photo © Daniel Zimmermann.

With over 100 stores, including over 20 restaurants and cafes on the souk's waterfront promenade, this is actually an interesting place to stop and have a lazy lunch followed with a strong Arabic coffee.

A good place to go check out after lunch is Gregg and Jane Sedgwick's Gallery One shop, which has exquisite pieces of art and stuff made by global artisans.

The Palace Resort

Many of the people who come to Downtown Dubai often ask themselves, "Where is the best place to stay?"

Well, that answer depends on your budget.

Photo © Guilhem Vellut.

One interesting hotel is **The Palace Downtown Dubai**, a five-star premium resort operated by The Address Hotels & Resorts. With 242 luxurious rooms, and 81 suites, you're treated to authentic Arabian interiors that give you incredible views of the Burj Lake, The Dubai Fountain or The Old Town Island.

If you can't stay there, at least go there to see!

Dubai Opera

At first sight you might wonder if **Dubai Opera** is not a mini version of the Sydney Opera House.

No, it is not.

Photo © Michael Mayer.

Actually the Dubai Opera is meant to look like a *dhow*, a traditional sailing vessel from that part of the world.

This performing arts center is nearly 65,000 square foot, and comes with 1901 seats, in multi-format. It opened in 2016 and had Spanish tenor Plácido Domingo as its first performer.

Like many buildings in Downtown Dubai, such as the Burj Khalifa and The Dubai Mall, Emaar Properties developed the Dubai Opera building.

AL QUOZ

If you're an art lover then the **Al Quoz** neighborhood is for you. This was a boring industrial neighborhood, but is now slowly being turned into the new Chelsea.

Photo © Peter Dowley.

What are some of the interesting artistic things you will find here? In Al Quoz you will find the region's first gallery for for contemporary Middle Eastern art, chic new concept cafes, and a chance to see nice street art.

Photo © Siska Maria Eviline.

Raw Cafe

Coffee lovers from all over the world agree that one of the best places to sip coffee is at **RAW Coffee Company** in the Al Quoz neighborhood.

Photo © Siska Maria Eviline.

The company says they roast and supply Dubai's only premium 100% locally roasted, 100% organic, and 100% ethically traded fresh Arabica coffee.

With cute hand-written slogans like "Life begins after coffee" and the kitten on its back saying "Just pour the coffee straight in," you will have a chuckle with your favorite coffee of the day.

Photo © Alserkal Avenue.

Art Spaces

Since 2007 Al Quoz has been slowly growing to become the art hub of the city. The heart of Al Quoz's art scene is the **Alserkal Avenue**, a cluster of architect-designed warehouses.

Photo © Alserkal Avenue.

Some of the artistic adventures you can have on this street include the **Salsali Private Museum (SPM),** which in 2011 opened as the first Private Museum for contemporary art in the region, the **La Galerie Nationale**, a gallery specialized in original art furniture made by top designers from the 20th century, as well as **Gulf Photo Plus (GPP),** the only dedicated center for photography in the city.

Photo © Guilhem Vellut.

THE BEACHES

The Arabian Gulf is home to some of the most beautiful crystal beaches on the planet. The coastline here, which is about 820 miles (or 1,318 KM), is serene. Think of it this way, about half of the country faces the Gulf. So, what are some of the beaches available to you?

The **Jumeirah Beach Park** is probably home to the most popular beach of the city. Because it is awarded the Blue Flag certification for adhering to strict international standards, and because it has great many facilities, it's popular with the tourists.

Locals might call it **Russian Beach**, and its actual name is JBR or Jumeirah Beach Residence, but this public beach is actually a fun place to go. It's popular with bathers, watersports such as parasailing, wakeboarding and banana boating are plenty, and it's a nice place to do a camel rides.

Then, of course, there is the **Umm Suqeim Beach**, which is well known for its views of the Burj Al Arab. There are services like jet skiing and fly-boarding. Some evenings you might even be treated to a yacht wedding.

"This is a historic beach," says Mark, a tourist, "It is a place to come because it has that Dubai landmark. I love coming here because there are less people, too."

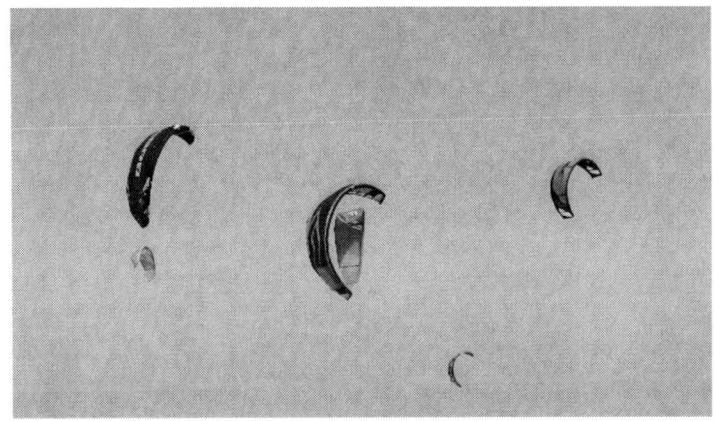

One of the more fun beaches of the city is **Kite Beach**, where kite surfers and spectators come together across from the Al Manara Road Junction. If you want to see incredible sport activities, head there to the late afternoons.

Al Sufouh Beach, also known as Black Palace Beach, is a very quiet beach. Located near the royal fortresses at Al Sufouh, for which it's named, it offers good views of Palm Jumeirah and the Burj Al Arab.

Sometime a **Hidden Beach** is all you need to discover on a trip. This beach sits on the left side of Sheraton Jumeirah if one is facing the waters. It truly is by far the best place to go for swimming, as there are hardly ever any people there, if you're looking for a safe and discreet way to enjoy swimming.

A friendly final note on beaches in Dubai is to keep yourself safe. Dubai Municipality rules state that a recreational fisherman should have a license before fishing in the specific areas where this is permitted.

If you're caught without a license, aside from the possibility of going to jail, you also pay a 1000 AED or about 275 USD.

If you're going to be here for long and would like one, the Environment Department in Deira does it. You will be given a "Recreational Fishing License" within about a week.

OLD DUBAI

Dubai is known for its skyscrapers, shoppers, and for being the Vegas of Arabia. However, did you know there is a part of the city that is actually ancient?

Old Town, or Old Dubai, is the place to experience the essence of Arabia. This part of town is home to well-known souks where gold, textiles, perfumes, and fish are sold.

Because Dubai is home to Africans, Arabs, a large number of other Asians, and western expats, its **Gold Souk** is one of the most versatile gold markets in the world, where 14, 18, 21, 22, and 24 karats are all easily available in many of the 300 jewelry shops at the market.

Again, because of its diversity, the **Spice Souk** offers all kinds of spices that are not easy to find in other cities of this size in the region. Spices from Zanzibar, Kerala, and even China are readily available to be tasted and tried.

One of the experiences every traveler should partake is crossing the Dubai creek on an **Abra**, which is the original form of transportation on these waters. These traditional boats will whisk you from one end of the creek to another for about 1 AED or about $0.25, on a one-way fare.

Humans have inhabited Dubai for at least 3000 years, as there is an archaeological evidence of nomadic cattle herders roaming the region. According to the Cleaner Ocean Foundation in the United Kingdom, the area that is now Dubai was covered in mangroves back in the 7000 BC, a fact only discovered the late 1990s as the city was expanding and the famous Al-Zayed Road was being constructed.

Although there is nothing really to help us tour any of that old history (outside of seeing the desert, which I will share later), we have to just accept the recent-ness of Dubai. As such, the oldest building of the Emirate is the **Al Fahidi Fort**, which only dates back to the 1700s.

This is a building that gives the traveler a chance to

jump back in time—a time in which the Bani Yas tribe coalition, which included the Dubai tribe of Al-Falasi, had ruled between parts of current day Saudi Arabia to Qatar.

Al Fahidi is importance for its historical remnants.

Photo © Elroy Serrao.

It is a majestic building, which used to be surrounded by several homes that resembled its architecture. Unfortunately, as Dubai was modernizing most of those buildings were destroyed. The city was planning a final destruction when a British architect named Rayner Otter campaigned the Royal family in the United Kingdom to intervene.

According to *Emirates*, the national airline, Otter was able to get Prince Charles to recommend the end the destructive plans of the city, which the Emir agreed to.

Other attractions to check out in Old Dubai include the must-see **Dubai Municipality Museum** in Deira, which records the modern historical evolution of the city, even

94

though the building itself is only dating back to the 1950s.

As you walk around these attractions you will see an Emirate that has had an incredible evolution in terms of its modern development.

Just imagine: until the 1990s Dubai used to look more like Old Dubai than the skyline you see today.

Photo © Robert Haandrikman.

THE DESERT

The Arabian Desert is incredible. Although Iraq, Jordan, Kuwait, Oman, Qatar, Saudi Arabia, United Arab Emirates and Yemen share this massive natural phenomenon, there is nowhere else that a tourist can freely explore the same way as it is here.

All you really have to do is get a car and a driver, and just go and explore!

Here there is such a thing as a **Desert Safari**, and it really is exactly as it sounds. It is not for everyone, but I think it is an experience one should not miss.

Because the UAE is generally pretty hot, I recommend dividing your desert exploring into different segments. For example, you could go on a morning safari, which normally lasts from eight in the morning to about noon. During that time, before it really gets hot, you will be able to visit the **Dunes**, which is best experienced with a four-wheeled taxi, as you will be thrown around in the car because your driver wants to make sure you all don't get stuck in the sand.

Photo © Bryn Pinzgauer.

In the meantime, if you're the adventurous type then you will love the Arabian Desert. There are tons of self-exploring methods, including renting bikes and just flying around the stuff.

"I had to actually get ready for my trip for months," said Moritz, a German tourist, "I had to learn how to ride a bike in this type of environment."

But, like the many people who do so, Moritz loved the experience, describing as a kind of rush he had never felt before in his life.

What are some of the other activities to do in the morning before it gets too hot?

What about sandboarding!

Photo © David Rogers.

One of the good things about desert sand is that it is around all year long. You don't have to wait until a particular season to do your favorite activities.

As such, unlike snowboarding, sandboarding is pretty much a thing you can do any time of the year.

"The only downside I can think of is that going back up sucks," laughed Nicole, an American tourist, noting the difficulty in setting up a dune lift (as opposed to "ski lift"), as she had to walk back up and forth. "You just get tired after a while because it is as though you're working out twice, which, of course, you are!"

Sanboarding enthusiasts like Nicole, however, don't

mind doing this. They're normally in great shape, and generally have a whole list of places they do this, including in Egypt, South Africa, and other parts of the world where there is enough sand dunes to do it.

Nevertheless, if your day activities lead you to tire then worry not as the desert makes up for it at night.

Photo © Bhavishya Goel.

The folks who live in the Arabian Desert, the Bedouin, know how to kick up entertaining storm in the evening. They set up tents, surrounded by fire and delicious local food, as they watch belly dancers and other types of entertainers take their mind off of that exhausting heat.

Hence, why I recommended up splitting up your visits. One day you could do your morning stuff, and another day you could go back in the late afternoon—to enjoy the incredible desert sunset, followed by nice food and fun.

What is the best way to do this?

Spend the night, of course, which any tour company can arrange for you, because you want to wake up to the sunrise of the Arabian Desert.

There is really nothing like it. The light of the sun reflects against the golden sand, which creates amazing colors on the sky, especially when a little bit cloudy.

It is a reminder that nature is so much more powerful than species, and I think the desert is a great place to have in mind, as you go back to your own life and nature.

Thanks Everyone

Thank you to all the people who helped made this book possible. Thank you to all the people of Dubai for their generosity.

If you want to get in touch please email me at: guidesbyadam@gmail.com or you can follow me on Social media (Instagram @GuidesByAdam or Twitter @GuidesByAdam).

You can also read my travel blog on Wordpress at GuidesByAdam.Wordpress.com

Thanks again!

ABOUT ADAM

Adam Jackson is a writer and traveler based in New York. His guidebooks are about locations he is passionate about. Other travel books by this author include *Zanzibar* and *The Ancestral Trip*, as well as the *Budget* series, which includes cities like Bangkok and New York.